MACDONALD STARTERS

Money

Wouah
yenoM

Macdonald Educational

About Macdonald Starters

Macdonald Starters are vocabulary controlled information books for young children. More than ninety per cent of the words in the text will be in the reading vocabulary of the vast majority of young readers. Word and sentence length have also been carefully controlled.

Key new words associated with the topic of each book are repeated with picture explanations in the Starters dictionary at the end. The dictionary can also be used as an index for teaching children to look things up.

Teachers and experts have been consulted on the content and accuracy of the books.

Illustrated by: Gary Long

Written and planned by: Diana Ferguson

Managing editor: Su Swallow

Production: Stephen Pawley, Vivienne Driscoll

Reading consultant: Donald Moyle, author of *The Teaching of Reading* and senior lecturer in education at Edge Hill College of Education

Chairman, teacher advisory panel: F. F. Blackwell, Director, Primary Extension Programme, National Council for Educational Technology; general inspector for schools (primary), London Borough of Croydon

Teacher panel: Loveday Harmer, Joy West, Enid Wilkinson

Series devised by: Peter Usborne

Colour reproduction by Paramount Litho Company

© Macdonald and Company (Publishers) Limited 1974
ISBN 0 356 04633 8
Made and printed in Great Britain by Purnell & Sons Limited
Paulton, Somerset

Filmset by Layton-Sun Limited

First published 1974 by Macdonald and Company (Publishers) Limited
St. Giles House
49-50 Poland Street
London W1A 2LG

These men are bank robbers.
They are stealing money from the bank.
They will drive off in a fast car.

1

Many people keep money in a bank.
This man is putting his money
in the bank.
2

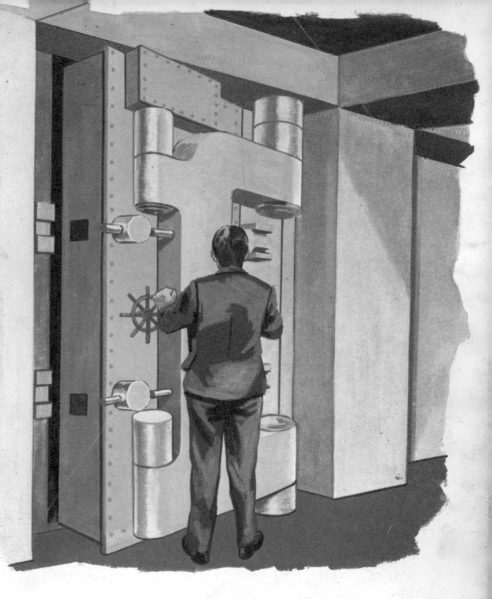

The money is put in a big safe.
The door of the safe is very strong.

It is pay day in this factory.
These men are bringing the money.

This man has got his pay packet.
He is counting his money.

This place is called a mint.
Coins are made here.
First, molten metal is put into moulds.

The metal gets hard.
Then it is rolled out like this.

blanks

This machine cuts out the coin shapes.
They are called blanks.
The blanks are made into coins.

8

Here is a machine
for printing paper mon
At first, the money loo   g for treasure.
Then it is cut up into r x of gold coins.
                          n ship.

Here is a wedding in Cyprus.
The bride and the bridegroom dance.
People pin money on to their clothes.

12

This lady wears coins around her head.
This shows that she is married.

Long ago there was no money.
People used all kinds of things instead.
This man is trading a cow
for some cloth.

14

Once, all these things were used
as money.

This man is printing
his own money.
This is against the law.

Some policemen have come
to arrest the man.

This man is a miser.
He never spends his money.
He hides it all away.

Here is a millionaire.
He is very rich.

Every country has its own money.
20

Here is some of the money
from different countries.

See for yourself
Put some paper over a coin.
Rub over it with a pencil.
See what happens.

Starter's **Money** words

bank
(page 1)

safe
(page 3)

robber
(page 1)

door
(page 3)

money
(page 1)

notes
(page 5)

car
(page 1)

coins
(page 5)

mint
(page 6)

paper money
(page 9)

metal
(page 7)

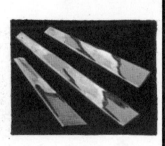

auction
(page 10)

roll
(page 7)

divers
(page 11)

blanks
(page 8)

treasure
(page 11)

24

ship
(page 11)

cow
(page 14)

wedding
(page 12)

arrest
(page 17)

bride
(page 12)

miser
(page 18)

bridegroom
(page 12)

millionaire
(page 19)